EXTREME SCIENCE

D1635487

MAGNIFICENT HABITATS

First published in Great Britain
in 2019 by Wayland
Copyright © Hodder and Stoughton, 2019
All rights reserved

Editor: Amy Pimperton
Text written by Rob Colson and
Jon Richards
Produced by Tall Tree Ltd
Designers: Malcolm Parchment and
Ben Ruocco

HB ISBN: 978 1 5263 0774 3
PB ISBN: 978 1 5263 0775 0

Wayland
An imprint of Hachette Children's Group
Part of Hodder and Stoughton
Carmelite House
50 Victoria Embankment
London EC4Y 0DZ

An Hachette UK Company
www.hachette.co.uk
www.hachettechildrens.co.uk

Printed in China

Picture credits:
Every attempt has been made to
clear copyright. Should there be any
inadvertent omission, please apply to
the publisher for rectification.

FSC
www.fsc.org
MIX
Paper from
responsible sources
FSC® C104740

CONTENTS

A WORLD OF HABITATS

Earth is covered in a rich variety of habitats. Each habitat is a different type of environment in which different organisms live. These range from the cold, icy regions around the poles to the scorching deserts at the Equator and down to the depths of the ocean floor.

29%

71%

Land makes up about **29%** of Earth's surface.

36%

31%

33%

Of this, **31%** is desert, **33%** is grassland **36%** is forest.

Furnace Creek, Death Valley, California, USA

North Atlantic Ocean

Pacific Ocean

South Atlantic Ocean

Habitat key

Ocean

Desert

Taiga

Tundra

Montane

Temperate grassland

Polar desert

Deciduous forest

Mediterranean vegetation

Tropical rainforest

Tropical grassland

EXTREMES ON EARTH

HOTTEST PLACE

The highest temperature ever recorded is **57.6°C**, at **Furnace Creek, Death Valley, California, USA**. The **Mojave fringe-toed lizard** lives there. When temperatures become too hot, the lizard 'swims' under the sand to find cooler conditions.

In the McMurdo Dry Valleys of Antarctica

NO RAIN OR SNOW

has fallen for nearly 2 million years.

The fringe-toed lizard has triangular fringes on its toes to stop it from sinking into the sand when it runs.

COLDEST PLACE

The lowest temperature ever recorded is **-89.2°C**, at **Vostok Station, Antarctica**. Vostok Station is also one of the sunniest places on Earth, with nearly **4,000 hours** of sunshine **per year**.

Arctic Ocean

Pacific Ocean

Meghalaya, India

Indian Ocean

Southern Ocean

Vostok Station, Antarctica

WETTEST PLACE

The state of **Meghalaya, India**, receives **12,000 mm** of rain per year. Most of the state is covered in dense forest, which supports a huge range of plants and animals, including the **hoolock gibbon**.

Hoolock gibbons spend most of their lives in trees. Males are black and females are brown.

OPEN AND DEEP OCEAN

The ocean is the largest habitat on Earth, covering about 71 per cent of the planet. About 92 per cent is open ocean. The remaining 8 per cent is formed by the continental shelf, with a depth of less than 200 metres.

OCEANS

The oceans have an average depth of **3,800 metres**. The very deepest part, **Challenger Deep** in the **Pacific Ocean**, plunges to **10,994 metres** below the surface. The **pressure** at this depth is nearly **1,100** times greater than at the surface and the temperature is just above **0°C**.

MARINE LIFE

Most life is found close to the **shoreline**. Away from the coasts the open ocean is like a watery desert, where living things are scattered far and wide.

Only about **10 per cent** of all marine species live in the open ocean. This is because there are very few nutrients in the water to support the **microscopic plankton** that form the basis of the ocean food chain. However, when nutrients do well up from the depths, they can cause explosions in the numbers of these tiny organisms. These create huge **blooms of algae** that can cover **hundreds** of **square kilometres**.

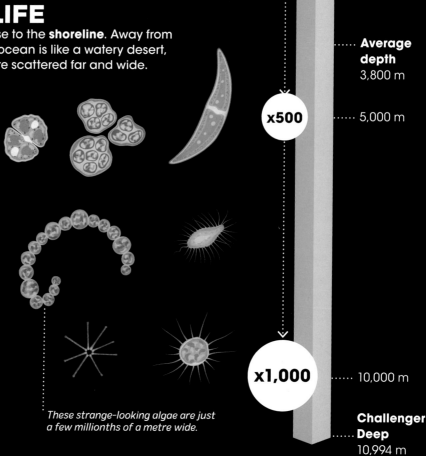

These strange-looking algae are just a few millionths of a metre wide.

Pressure

Surface

1,000 m

Average depth
3,800 m

x500

5,000 m

x1,000

10,000 m

Challenger Deep
10,994 m

OCEAN GIANTS

Some huge animals cruise the world's oceans, including the largest animal that has ever lived, the blue whale.

Blue whales are endangered. There are only about **25,000** of them left in the wild.

Blue whale: 30 metres long

Whale shark: 13 metres long

Giant squid: 12 metres long

The solitary giant oarfish is rarely spotted. It is thought to be the source of tales about fearsome **SEA SERPENTS** that appear in the ancient myths of the Greeks and the Vikings.

Giant oarfish: 11 metres long

HYDROTHERMAL VENTS

Found close to volcanically active regions, **hydrothermal vents** are underwater fountains of **super-hot**, **mineral-rich** water. They support large communities of organisms, including tube worms, bacteria and eels. Water at these vents has been recorded at temperatures of more than **450°C**, but it doesn't boil because the pressure at these depths is so high.

Riftia pachyptila, *or giant tube worms*

Kiwa hirsuta *is a crustacean that lives around hydrothermal vents in the South Pacific Ocean. It has been nicknamed the yeti lobster for its hairy legs.*

COASTAL HABITATS

Close to land, conditions change regularly as the tide moves up and down the shore and where rivers flow into the sea, carrying fresh water and huge amounts of sediment. These regions are teeming with life as ocean currents bring nutrients to create a rich habitat.

HIGH TIDE

Gravitational forces from the Sun and Moon pull on the waters of the ocean, causing the tides to rise and fall each day. The greatest tidal range is found at the **Bay of Fundy** in Canada, where the waters rise and fall by as much as **15 metres** with each tide. That's the average height of a four-storey building.

Tidal range 15 m

ROCK POOLS

At low tide, pools form in rocks on the shore. These shallow rock pools provide a refuge for creatures to survive until high tide. Creatures you might find in a rock pool include **starfish, sea anemones** and **hermit crabs**. Starfish and sea anemones are animals with no **brain**, **heart** or **blood**.

Sea anemones have stinging tentacles that they use to catch tiny plankton.

When they eat, **starfish** can eject their stomachs out of their bodies to collect food, which they then suck back in.

Hermit crabs live inside shells that they find on the seabed.

TOUGH TEETH

Limpets are shellfish that feed by scouring rocks. A limpet's **teeth** are the strongest known biological substance and are capable of scraping off pieces of rock.

At low tide, limpets cling tightly to rocks. This stops the limpets from drying out.

On a beach, buried beneath every square metre of sand, there may be as many as

2,000 SHELLFISH

hiding in burrows, waiting for the tide to return.

OCEAN MEADOWS

The nutrients in coastal regions lead to the growth of several rich habitats, such as **kelp forests** and **seagrass meadows**. These places support a wide range of plant and animal life and protect coastal areas from **erosion**.

Some species of kelp can grow up to **60 cm** in a single day!

Manatee

Giant kelp: up to **30 metres**

Manatees are large mammals that spend their days grazing on seagrass in tropical coastal waters. They can grow up to

4 M LONG.

VAST GRASS

Seagrass meadows are thought to make up about **15 per cent** of the ocean's ability to store carbon.

SALTY FORESTS

Mangrove swamps are coastal habitats where plants and animals have evolved to cope with the salty conditions, which can be more than twice as salty as normal seawater.

Mudskippers are **amphibious fish** that live in mangrove swamps. They can walk on land by **pulling** themselves along with their fins.

CORAL REEFS

Coral reefs are some of the richest habitats on the planet. They support at least 25 per cent of all sea species and can stretch for thousands of kilometres. These huge structures are formed from the dead bodies of tiny creatures.

TINY BUILDERS

Coral reefs are built by colonies of tiny organisms called **coral polyps**. These polyps form a hard outer **exoskeleton** for protection. When the polyp dies, the exoskeleton remains and more polyps grow on top of it. Over thousands of years, the exoskeletons build up to form a **reef**.

Coral polyp

GREAT BARRIER REEF

The **Great Barrier Reef** off the north-east coast of Australia is the largest coral reef in the world, stretching for about **2,300 km**. It started to form about **6,000** years ago and is home to about **9,000** marine species:

- 6 species of **marine turtles**
- 30 species of **marine mammals**
- 100 species of **jellyfish**
- 215 species of **birds**
- 133 species of **rays** and **sharks**

- 500 species of **worms**
- 1,300 species of **crustaceans**
- 1,625 species of **fish**
- 2,000 species of **sponges**
- 3,000+ species of **molluscs**.

THE GREAT BARRIER REEF IS THE ONLY LIVING STRUCTURE VISIBLE FROM **SPACE.**

BARRIER REEF LIFE

Gulls nest on nearby land, and come to the reef to catch fish.

Rays stay close to the ocean floor as they feed.

Jellyfish are attracted to the warm tropical water.

Dolphins visit the reef to feed on the many fish found there.

SEX CHANGER

The **humphead wrasse** is a large fish found in coral reefs. Some **female** wrasse can change into males when they are around **9 years** old. The males grow up to **2 metres** long, twice as long as the females, and have even bigger humps on their heads.

THE HUMPHEAD WRASSE IS ALSO KNOWN AS THE **NAPOLEON WRASSE.**

Male wrasse

Female wrasse

Whale shark

ANNUAL FEAST

Every year, the corals release huge clouds of **eggs** and **sperm** in a mass **spawning** event. This attracts a huge amount of wildlife that feed off the eggs, including the biggest fish in the sea, the **whale shark**.

Coral reefs are under threat from **rising** sea temperatures, caused by global warming. This **bleaches** the coral and may even kill it. According to some studies, up to **60 per cent** of the world's coral reefs are under threat from climate change caused by humans.

Coral eggs

Bleached coral

Turtles come to the Barrier Reef to mate and nest.

Giant clams can live for more than 100 years.

Sponges are simple brainless animals that feed by allowing water to flow through them.

Fan worm

Bristle worms are predators on the ocean floor.

Green turtles feed on seagrass.

Clams stay in one place and feed on passing plankton.

Sea worms on the reef come in many shapes, sizes and colours.

NORTHERN FORESTS

Stretching right across the northern parts of Asia, Europe and North America is an enormous band of forest. Known as taiga or boreal forest, it makes up the largest habitat on land and accounts for as much as 29 per cent of Earth's forests.

HARSH CONDITIONS

Conditions in **boreal forests** can be very harsh, with long, cold winters and short summers.

+18°C -20°C

Summer average high

...... Winter average high

TEMPERATURE RANGE

It can be warm in the brief summer, sometimes reaching **30°C**, but temperatures plunge below **-50°C** in winter.

The growing season is very short and can last as little as
50 DAYS
in some areas.

In the depths of winter, daylight can last for just **5 hours**.

Sun rising at 9.30 a.m. and setting at 2.30 p.m.

TOUGH TREES

Evergreen trees dominate the forests. They have **thin, needle-like** leaves that are tough enough to survive the cold conditions and **reduce** water loss. The leaves stay on **all year round** so that the tree can make enough food during the short winter days to survive.

The needles on fir trees are attached to the branches in clusters.

SURVIVING THE EXTREMES

Animals that live in these cold regions have special **adaptations** to **survive** when conditions get tough.

The caribou is known in Europe as the **REINDEER**. In northern Finland, the Sami people survive by migrating with their herds of reindeer.

Caribou grow thick, woolly fur in winter. The fur thins out during the summer.

Caribou hooves are wide to stop the animals sinking into the snow. They have sharp edges to help grip ice and rocks.

Wolf

13

MIGRATING HERDS

Porcupine caribou take part in the longest land animal migrations in North America. Huge herds of more than **200,000** animals walk more than **2,400 kilometres** each year across northern Canada and Alaska.

Wolves hunt large prey, such as caribou, by working together in packs. Like their prey, the wolves' winter fur keeps them warm even when temperatures drop to **-40°C**.

HIBERNATION

Some animals **hibernate** during the winter months, slowing down their metabolism (the rate their bodies work at) to preserve energy. Brown bears eat as much as they can in summer. During their winter hibernation, they lose about half their body weight.

Fattened ready for hibernation

Emaciated after long hibernation

TEMPERATE FORESTS

Further away from the poles than boreal forests, temperate forests are found in the world's temperate regions, where conditions are milder.

Beech
deciduous

Pine
evergreen

FOUR SEASONS

Warmer winters, four distinct seasons and regular rainfall mean that temperate forests can include a mixture of **deciduous** and **evergreen** trees.

MILD AND WET

The temperature range is narrow, changing by about **10–20°C** through the year. Rainfall measures between **75–150 cm** per year.

While **evergreen** trees keep their leaves all year round, **deciduous** trees lose their leaves each year. In autumn, the green **chlorophyll** in their leaves breaks down. The leaves turn from green into a range of browns, reds, oranges and yellows, before dropping off.

Spring

Summer

Winter

Autumn

In autumn, fallen leaves cover the forest floor, creating a layer called **leaf litter**. As it **rots**, it releases nutrients into the soil.

Leaf litter is also a source of food for **slugs**, **snails**, **woodlice**, **beetles** and other **bugs**.

LIFE IN AN OAK TREE

A large deciduous tree, such as an **oak**, can support a huge variety of living things.

Many animals feed off the oak's **acorns** and **leaves**, including **squirrels**, **bears**, **magpies** and **insects**.

These animals attract others who may feed off them, such as insect-eating birds, including **warblers** and **orioles**.

The tree can also provide shelter for animals, including **tawny owls** and **ring-tailed cats**, while some insects, such as **wasps**, lay their eggs on it.

Some bugs are found living in and under its bark, including **spiders** and **centipedes**, while **nematodes** and **earthworms** can be found among its roots.

Orioles breed during the summer in northern temperate forests.

Tawny owl

Spiders feed on termites and other invertebrates.

Black bear

Salamanders hide from predators under logs.

Even dead oak trees are useful to wildlife, as **salamanders, worms** and **termites** live in them, breaking down the dead wood and returning the nutrients to the soil.

RAINFORESTS

These lush habitats are found in wet parts of the world, both in the tropics and in temperate regions. A huge variety of plants and animals live here, adapted to the warm and wet conditions.

TROPICAL RAINFORESTS

Tropical rainforests cover just 6 per cent of Earth's land surface, but the plants growing there produce about 28 per cent of the world's oxygen by photosynthesis.

Out of more than 10 million species of plants and animals that have been identified by scientists on Earth, more than half of them live in tropical rainforests.

LAYERED LIFE

Plants in the rainforest grow in four distinct layers.

Emergents: the tallest poke out of the top of the canopy, reaching up to 70 metres.

Canopy: this is the main tree level in a rainforest, forming a continuous layer of foliage that reaches about 50 metres.

Under canopy: this is made up of smaller trees.

A **raindrop** can take **10 minutes** to drip from the thick canopy to the forest floor.

Shrub and forest floor: with very little light, only small, short plants are found here.

VAST AMAZON

The **Amazon Rainforest** in South America covers a vast area of **5.5 million square kilometres**. It is so big that, if it were a separate country, it would be the **seventh** biggest in the world – bigger than the whole of **India**.

India has an area of 3.3 million square kilometres.

GROWING ON TREES

Rainforest plants called **epiphytes**, such as **orchids**, do not grow on the ground. Instead, they grow out of trees.

PLANTS

The Teresensis' bromeliad treefrog lays its eggs in pools that form inside the leaves of bromeliad plants. The **tadpoles** hatch and grow into adult frogs before leaving the pool.

Tadpoles

17

Bromeliads are a large group of plants that includes the pineapple.

SHRINKING FORESTS

Rainforests are cleared to make room for human **settlements, mines, farms** and **plantations**. An area the size of a **football pitch** is cleared every single second. **Twenty per cent** of the Amazon Rainforest has already disappeared.

22,500 KM² – AN AREA THE SIZE OF THE US STATE OF **NEW JERSEY** – DISAPPEARS EVERY YEAR.

TEMPERATE RAINFORESTS

These are found in **cooler** parts of the world, such as **North America, East Asia** and **Australia**. Temperate rainforests have two distinct seasons: a **wet** season and a **dry** season. Some of the largest living things on the planet are found here. **Giant redwoods** in California can grow to more than **100 metres** in height – taller than the **Statue of Liberty**.

Statue of Liberty

92.99 m

TEMPERATE GRASSLANDS

All of the world's continents, except for Antarctica, have large areas of grassland. Temperate grassland regions are found in cooler areas away from the tropics. These vast habitats are home to enormous groups of animals.

SEASONS

Temperate grasslands experience **four** seasons each year (**spring, summer, autumn** and **winter**) with temperatures ranging from **-10°C** in winter to **28°C** in summer. They usually receive between **30–60 cm** of rain a year.

Atlantic Ocean

Pacific Ocean

Indian Ocean

■ **Temperate grassland**   ■ **Tropical grassland**

MANY NAMES

Temperate grasslands have different names around the world:

NORTH AMERICA
PRAIRIES

SOUTH AMERICA
PAMPAS

CENTRAL EUROPE AND ASIA
STEPPE

Subsoil is a mixture of sand and clay under the roots.

Roots take water and minerals from the soil.

Some grasses grow to **7 metres tall** and send roots down **2 metres** to find moisture.

CLEVER CRITTERS

Prairie dogs are **rodents** that live in huge **underground burrows** called towns. The biggest town ever found was in **Texas**. It covered about **65,000 square kilometres** and was home to about **400 million prairie dogs**.

Prairie dogs warn each other when predators approach. They have **different** calls for different predators, such as **coyotes**, **eagles** or even **humans**. They also describe the **size** and **colour** of the predator, so their call for a human in a **red** T-shirt will be different from their call for a human in a **blue** T-shirt.

65,000 KM² IS AN AREA THE SIZE OF THE US STATE OF **WEST VIRGINIA.**

Prairie dogs are a type of **GROUND SQUIRREL** found in the United States, Canada and Mexico.

One dog barks a warning.

Prairie dogs watch vigilantly.

Potential threat

Bison roam in separate herds of males and females.

In the USA, the bison is also known as the **BUFFALO.**

DISAPPEARING BISON

The prairies once supported huge herds of **bison**. There were **tens** of **millions** of them at the start of the **1800s**. During the next **100 years**, hunters killed an estimated **50 million** bison, reducing their numbers to fewer than **1,000** throughout the whole of **North America** by 1889. Today, they have recovered to about **200,000**.

Wildfires are important in grassland areas. They stop large trees from growing, but grasses can grow back because, unlike many other plants, they grow from their **bases** or even parts that lie below the soil. Fire may destroy the top of the grass, but the growing part survives and the grass regrows.

Wildfires spread swiftly in dry summers.

TROPICAL GRASSLANDS

Tropical grasslands cover huge areas of Africa and are also found in India, Nepal, Australia and parts of the Americas. Warmer than temperate grasslands, they also receive a lot more rainfall.

WET AND DRY

Temperatures range from **15°C** to **35°C** and the grasslands can receive up to **150 cm** of rain a year. There are two distinct seasons each year: a **wet season** when rainfall is high, and a **dry season** when the rains stop.

SERENGETI

The Serengeti in **Tanzania** and **Kenya** in East Africa is one of the richest grassland habitats. It is home to **70** large mammal species, including **lions**, **giraffes** and **wildebeest**, and **500 bird** species. It is also the region where some of the oldest fossils of our human ancestors have been found.

.....The fossils found in the Serengeti suggest that humans first evolved here.

MIGRATIONS

During the wet season, food is abundant, but dry seasons bring drought and water shortages. This forces the **huge herds** of **plant-eating** animals to migrate to wetter areas where the rains are still falling.

Every year in **East Africa**, a huge herd containing **1.5 million wildebeest, 200,000 zebras** and thousands of antelope migrate in search of food and water.

Crocodiles lie in wait for the migrating wildebeest.

During their migration, wildebeest must cross crocodile-infested rivers.

SAVING WATER

Many plants in tropical grasslands are **xerophytic**, which means that they are adapted to cope with periods when **little** or **no** rain falls. For example, **acacia** trees have small, waxy leaves that minimise water loss and thorns to protect them from plant-eating animals.

Baobab trees store water in their trunks and have thick bark to protect them from grassland fires.

Baobab

Acacia

Acacias and baobabs are found in Africa and Australia.

Australian tropical grasslands are home to many large animals, including the **red kangaroo** and the **emu**, both of which can stand up to **2 metres** tall.

Human ...

Red kangaroo ...

Emu ...

Emu and Kangaroo: up to **2 m**

The Great Wildebeest Migration has been called one of the

SEVEN NEW WONDERS OF THE WORLD.

This annual event happens between the Serengeti National Park in Tanzania and the Maasai Mara National Reserve in Kenya.

RIVERS AND WETLANDS

As rain falls on Earth's surface, it collects to form streams and rivers that merge and flow into lakes, swamps and other wetland areas. This fresh water and the nutrients carried in it create habitats that teem with life.

MIGHTY RIVER

At **6,400 km** long, the **Amazon** is the second-longest river in the world, but it is by far the largest in terms of volume of water. It drains a basin that covers **2.7 million square kilometres**, an area the same size as **Kazakhstan**. The Amazon carries about **20 per cent** of all the water that runs off Earth's surface.

During the wet season, the Amazon swells to more than three times its size, covering an area of **35,000 square km** and flooding the surrounding land.

Amazon Basin

Rio Negro

Amazon

Many other large rivers flow into the Amazon, including the Rio Negro – the seventh largest river in the world by volume.

EVERGLADES

The Everglades is a large area of tropical wetlands in south Florida, USA, and includes a mix of **fresh** and **saltwater** areas. It is home to more than **200,000 alligators**, which can grow more than **4 metres long**. They hunt other **reptiles**, **birds** and **mammals**, but luckily for us they mostly avoid humans.

It has recently been discovered that, as well as eating meat, alligators like to munch on a variety of fruits.

Although they are easily capable of killing a human, alligator attacks in the Everglades are rare.

INLAND DELTA

The **Okavango Delta** is a huge inland delta in **Botswana**, Africa. This region covers about **15,000 square km** and is very flat, only varying in height by about **2 metres**. Every year, some **11 cubic km** of water flows into the area, flooding it. Large animals, such as **elephants and zebra**, come to the delta to feed on the plants that grow there. Predators, such as **lions**, **cheetahs** and **crocodiles**, lie in wait for them.

Botswana has the largest elephant population in Africa, with more than

135,000

Individuals.

INTO THE DEEP

Great Slave Lake, **Canada: 614 m**

Crater Lake, **USA: 594 m**

Loch Ness, **Scotland: 227 m**

Lake Baikal, **Russia: 1,620 m**

DEPTH IN METRES

500 metres

1,000 metres

1,500 metres

2,000 metres

Burj Khalifa, Dubai, UAE: **830 m to tip**

DEEPEST LAKE

Lake Baikal in Russia is the **largest** freshwater lake in the world and the **deepest** continental body of water. Plunging to a depth of **1,620 metres**, it is deep enough to hold nearly two **Burj Khalifa skyscrapers** on top of each other!

Lake Baikal formed **30 million** years ago from a rift valley, where two continental plates moved apart. It holds about **20 per cent** of the world's surface freshwater, which is more than all of the North American **Great Lakes** combined.

More than **80 per cent** of the animals that live in Lake Baikal, such as the **Baikal seal** and the **Baikal oilfish**, are found nowhere else.

The Baikal seal is one of the smallest seals in the world, growing to a maximum of 1.5 m long.

The Baikal oilfish is the main source of food for the Baikal seal. It is very hard to catch, so humans do not generally eat it.

DESERTS

Deserts are the driest places on the planet, but don't think they're all scorching hot, sand-covered habitats. Some are stoney wastelands, while others are found at the coldest places on Earth. The plants and animals that live here need special adaptations to cope with the harsh conditions.

DRY PLACES

Deserts are places that receive less than **250 mm** of precipitation in a year. Temperatures vary from desert to desert, reaching above **50°C** or plunging well below **freezing**.

HOT DESERTS

The largest **hot** desert is the **Sahara** in North Africa, which covers about **9 million square km**.

Across the whole world, about

230,000 SQUARE METRES

of land is turning to desert (a process called desertification) every single minute.

COLD DESERTS

The largest **cold** desert (and the largest desert of any kind) is **Antarctica**, which covers about **14 million square km**.

Antarctica is the coldest, windiest, highest and driest continent on **EARTH.**

ATACAMA

The **Atacama Desert** in Chile, South America, is formed in a rain shadow. Warm air blowing in from the **Pacific Ocean** contains plenty of water. As the air hits the Andes Mountains, it is **forced up** where it **cools**. As it gets **colder**, it **can't** hold on to the **water**, which falls as rain. The now dry air continues over the mountains, creating a dry rain shadow area on the other side.

The Atacama is the driest warm desert on Earth. Average rainfall is about **15 mm** a year.

Soil samples from the Atacama Desert are very similar to samples collected on **MARS.**

EXTREME SURVIVORS

Few animals can survive in the Atacama Desert. The **Chilean mouse opossum** is active mainly around dusk, when temperatures are falling.

Chilean mouse opossum

DESERT PLANTS

Cactuses are plants that are specially adapted to desert conditions. The thick succulent stems **hold on to water**. Their spines are modified leaves. They help to keep the plant cool by producing thousands of tiny shadows that protect it from the intense glare of the Sun.

Cactuses range in size from just 1 centimetre tall to nearly 20 metres in height.

EATING DUNG

Dung beetles do not drink at all. They get all the water they need from the animal poo that they eat.

Dung beetles roll balls of dung by pushing them with their hind legs.

DESERT ANIMALS

When animals find water in a desert, they need to make the most of it. A camel can drink up to **200 litres** of water in just three minutes. It can then go up to **10 days** without drinking at all.

By storing fat in its hump, a camel will stay cooler than if it had a thin layer of fat all around its body.

A spencer's burrowing frog survives in the **Australian** desert by **sleeping** under the sand. It stays there until **rains arrive**, at which point it **awakes** and climbs to the surface to feed and to mate.

Spencer's burrowing frog

MOUNTAINS

As mountains rise high into the air, conditions and climate change – as does the habitat. This creates distinct bands of habitats, each with their own types of plant and animal life.

CLIMATE ZONES

Mountains may have some or all of the below climate zones, each forming a distinct habitat with its own flora and fauna.

-6.5°C

Temperatures drop by up to **6.5°C** for every **1,000 metres** climbed.

Snow line ....very few things grow or live above this altitude
Nival zone ....only mosses and lichens grow here
Alpine zone ....consists of grass meadows
Treeline..uppermost limit where trees grow
Subalpine zone....................................contains coniferous forests
Montane zone.............a mix of deciduous and coniferous forests
Foothills zone.....................................consists of deciduous forests

KILIMANJARO

Just 300 kilometres south of the Equator, Mount Kilimanjaro is the **highest mountain in Africa**. It is **5,895 metres** tall. As you climb the mountain, you pass through many different habitats, from the baking hot bushland at its base to the permanent ice cap above 5,000 metres.

5,895 m

Snow line — Permanent snow – no plants or large animals ....

5,000 m

Nival zone — Moss and lichen........ ....Insects and spiders

4,000 m

Alpine zone — Grasses and heather...... ....Shrews

2,800 m

Montane zone — Dense jungle...... ....Colobus monkeys

1,800 m

Foothills zone — Coffee........ ....Humans

800 m

MOUNTAIN ANIMALS

Animals that live on mountains have to cross difficult terrain. As a result, large mountain creatures, such as the **chamois** and **mountain sheep,** are extremely agile and sure-footed.

Mountain animals also have to cope with extreme cold. Many of them, including **mountain leopards, llamas** and **chinchillas,** have developed thick coats to beat the chill.

People use llama wool for clothing because it is light, warm and water-repellent.

The **RINGS** on a mountain goat's horns can tell you its age in years, which is the number of rings minus one!

The chamois is a species of goat-antelope found in the European Alps. Quick and sure-footed, it can reach speeds of up to 50 km/h on the uneven rocky terrain.

Bearded vulture

27

Snow leopards have huge paws that act as snowshoes to keep them from sinking into the snow.

BONE COLLECTOR

The **bearded vulture** lives in the mountains of Europe, Asia and Africa. It feeds almost entirely on the **bones** of dead animals, taking its **nutrients** from the bone marrow. Bearded vultures have been seen on **Mount Everest** at altitudes of more than **7,000 metres.**

HUMAN IMPACT

People moving into highland areas to settle and farm land have reduced the size of wild habitats and the numbers of animals that live there. In the mountains of Central Asia, there are now as few as **4,000 snow leopards** left in the wild.

A bearded vulture's stomach contains extra-strong acid to break down bone.

TUNDRA AND THE POLES

The extreme north and south of the planet are covered in cold, frozen regions. Temperatures are so low that the ground is either permanently frozen all-year round, restricting plant life, or covered in thick layers of ice and snow, stopping plant life from growing at all.

THE POLES

The ice sheet covering Antarctica is nearly **4,800 metres** deep at its thickest.

About **95 per cent** of the continent is covered with ice.

Earth is tilted in its orbit, which means that the regions around the poles experience **24 hours** of sunlight a day during the height of summer, and **24 hours** of **darkness** in the depths of winter.

Sun

DECEMBER
- winter in the Northern Hemisphere
- summer in the Southern Hemisphere

Tilt: 23.5°

JUNE
- summer in the Northern Hemisphere
- winter in the Southern Hemisphere

APEX PREDATOR

In the Arctic, the polar bear is the apex (top) predator. To cope with the extreme cold, **polar bears** have:

- **fur** on the soles of their feet to insulate them against the ice
- **large feet** to grip on the ice and swim through the water
- **sharp teeth** and **claws** to catch prey quickly
- **thick fur** to insulate the body and camouflage the animal against the snow
- **thick layers** of **fat**, or **blubber**, for warmth.

Polar bears are champion swimmers, able to cover more than **100 KM** without stopping.

DIGGING DOWN

In the long winter, most of the ground is covered with deep snow. Grazing animals have to dig through the snow to find food.

TUNDRA

Tundra comes from the Finnish word 'tuntria', meaning 'treeless land'.

The Arctic tundra in the far north is covered in snow for about eight months each year.

During winter, caribou dig lichen out from under the snow for food.

PERMAFROST

Below the surface of the tundra regions is a thick layer of permanently frozen soil, called **permafrost**.

At its deepest, this permafrost can reach down to **1,450 metres**. The frozen soil stops plants with deep roots from growing and prevents animals digging deep burrows for shelter.

SUMMER

In summer months, rising temperatures in the tundra cause the very top layer of the soil to thaw, plants to **grow** and **bloom** and insects to hatch. This eruption of life attracts migrating animals, including flocks of birds, such as **snow geese**.

The plants that bloom during summer in the Arctic tundra include bearberries, cushion plants and the Arctic willow.

Snow geese arrive in the Arctic tundra every spring. They nest and raise young before flying south for the winter.

GLOSSARY

ALGAE
Tiny plants that grow in water and lack stems, roots or leaves.

ALGAL BLOOM
The rapid growth in the number of tiny marine organisms. Some of these blooms are so big that they can be seen from space.

AMPHIBIOUS
Able to live both on land and in water.

BARK
The tough outer covering of a tree. It protects the inner parts of the trunk and branches, reducing water loss and preventing damage caused by animals.

CRUSTACEANS
A type of animal that has a hard outer shell and several pairs of legs. They include crabs.

DELTA
A triangle-shaped area of sand and soil deposited at the mouth of some large rivers.

DESERT
The name given to a region that receives less than 250 mm of precipitation (rain, snow or hail) in a year. Deserts can be hot, such as the Sahara, or cold, such as Antarctica.

EQUATOR
An imaginary circle around the Earth halfway between the North Pole and the South Pole.

EROSION
The gradual wearing away of soil or the Earth's surface by wind, rain or another natural substance.

HABITAT
This is the natural environment in which a living thing lives.

HIBERNATION
A sleep-like state that many animals enter during cold periods. Their body actions slow down, saving energy when food and water may be in short supply.

HYDROTHERMAL VENTS
Holes in the seabed through which gushes super-hot water that is rich in minerals.

INVERTEBRATE
A type of animal that does not have a backbone. Invertebrates include insects and soft-bodied animals, such as octopuses.

MAMMAL
A type of warm-blooded animal that has a body covered with hair and that produces milk to feed its young.

MIGRATION
The regular movement of animals from one place to another, usually in search of food, water, or a place to give birth.

NUTRIENTS
Substances found in food that help animals, people and plants live and grow.

ORGANISM
A living thing, such as an animal, plant or bacteria.

OXYGEN
A colourless, odourless gas that is used by all living things to produce energy.

PAMPAS
A large area of grassland found in South America.

PHOTOSYNTHESIS
The process by which plants use sunlight, carbon dioxide and water to produce sugars and release oxygen into the air.

POLES
The most northern and southern points on the Earth are known as the North Pole and the South Pole ('the poles').

PRAIRIE
A large area of grassland found in North America.

RAINFOREST
A forested region that receives a lot of rain all year round.

SEDIMENT
Material carried by wind or water that settles on the sea- or riverbed or the surface of the land.

SPECIES
A group of living things that look and behave in the same way and produce fertile young that can have young of their own.

STEPPE
A large area of grassland that stretches from Eastern Europe and across Asia.

TAIGA
The name given to a large band of forest that stretches across northern parts of Asia, Europe and North America.

TEMPERATE
The name given to parts of the world that lie nearer the poles than the tropical regions.

TROPICAL
The name given to parts of the world that lie near the Equator.

TUNDRA
Huge, treeless plains found in the Arctic regions of North America, Europe and Asia.

INDEX